FEATHERED DINOSAURS

By Christopher Sloan

Introduction by Dr. Philip J. Currie

NATIONAL GEOGRAPHIC SOCIETY

WASHINGTON, D.C.

Copyright © 2000
Christopher Sloan

Published by the National
Geographic Society
1145 17th St. N.W.
Washington, D.C. 20036-4688

John M. Fahey, Jr.
President and Chief Executive Officer

Gilbert M. Grosvenor
Chairman of the Board

Nina D. Hoffman
Senior Vice President

William R. Gray
*Vice President and
Director of the Book Division*

Staff for this book

Nancy Laties Feresten
*Publishing Director, Children's Books
and Project Editor*

Suzanne Patrick Fonda
Editor

Jennifer Emmett
Associate Editor

Jo H. Tunstall
Editorial Assistant

Marianne R. Koszorus
Art Director, Children's Books

Lewis R. Bassford
Production Manager

Vincent P. Ryan
Manufacturing Manager

Elisabeth MacRae-Bobynsky
Indexer

Design by Christopher Sloan

Library of Congress
Cataloging-in-Publication
Numbers: 00-927001

ISBN 0-7922-7219-6

Cover: A model of the dinosaur
Deinonychus, which may have
had feathers.

Acknowledgments

Without the contributions of many
knowledgeable and talented
individuals this book would not
have been possible. I thank Lou
Mazzatenta for his photographs of
important new fossils; Brian Cooley
for his models of feathered
dinosaurs; and Dr. Gregory Paul,
whose drawings are sprinkled
throughout this book. I also thank
Dr. Alan Brush, Dr. Luis Chiappe,
Dr. Philip J. Currie, Dr. Kevin
Padian, and Dr. Hans Dieter Sues
for their valuable comments on the
text and graphics.

I would also like to acknowledge the
many institutions and scientists
around the world who generously
shared their fossils—and their
knowledge about them—with me.
I am especially indebted to the
National Geological Museum of
China, the Institute of Vertebrate
Paleontology and Paleoanthropology
in Beijing, China, and the
Paleontological Center of the
Mongolian Academy of Sciences.

In addition, I would like to thank my
wife, Portia, for her artwork and
support during this project as well as
my children, Andrew and Jessica,
who reviewed the book many times
to make sure it was cool. I would also
like to thank my colleague at
NATIONAL GEOGRAPHIC, Kurt
Mutchler, for his support and
thoughtful comments.

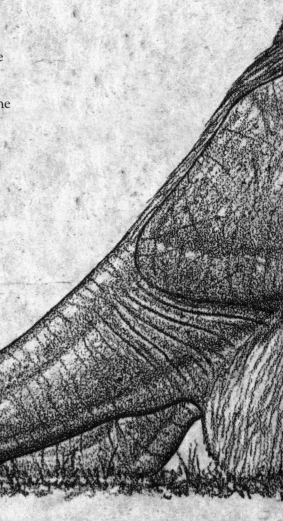

Contents

Introduction

When I was six years old, I never imagined that my love of dinosaurs would lead to an exciting career hunting for their fossils and trying making sense of them. There is little as satisfying, however, as making a prediction and seeing it come true.

More than 125 years ago, it was first proposed that dinosaurs were the direct ancestors of birds. The theory was not widely accepted until a quarter of a century ago. Some bold scientists even speculated that eventually we would find dinosaurs with feathers. I felt they were right, but feathers fossilize so rarely that it was beyond my wildest dreams to think *I* would ever see a feathered dinosaur. It was one of the greatest thrills in my career when I looked at the first *Sinosauropteryx* in China in 1996.

Although the evidence supporting dinosaurian ancestry is overwhelmingly based on similarities of bones, finding feathers and feather-like structures on dinosaurs had a greater impact on most people than a hundred skeletal characteristics shared by birds and dinosaurs. The strength of a prediction coming true has convinced most paleontologists that dinosaurs did not become extinct 65 million years ago. They are still alive and well in their descendants—the birds!

Dr. Philip J. Currie

Sinosauropteryx (right) was the first fossil of a dinosaur found with a feather-like skin covering. Even before this 1996 discovery, many scientists had concluded that birds descended from dinosaurs.

The Dinosaur-Bird Connection

There's a dinosaur in your backyard! That's what scientists who study dinosaurs might say if they saw a blue jay or a cardinal near your bird feeder. Why? Because within the last few years, amazing new discoveries suggest that all dinosaurs did not die out 65 million years ago. Some are flying around us today—as birds!

In the late 1860s, the British scientist Thomas Henry Huxley was the first to recognize that the bones of certain dinosaurs were similar to the bones of birds. Their hipbones and leg bones looked alike, and so did their skulls, feet, and many other parts of their skeletons.

The dinosaur bones scientists studied were fossils. Fossils are traces of prehistoric life that have been preserved in the earth. Sometimes fossils are the bony remains of long-dead animals. Other times fossils are just footprints or teeth. The fossils studied by scientists in the mid-1800s were mostly bones. These fossils formed when dinosaurs died and were buried in mud or sand for millions of

When bones of dinosaurs were found in the 1800s, few scientists imagined that birds, like this songbird shown perched on a dinosaur fossil, might be closely related to them.

When scientists first found dinosaur bones, they imagined dinosaurs were big, slow-moving lizards like these early dinosaur models made for a London park.

years. During that time, minerals slowly filled in all the tiny spaces within the bones and turned them to stone.

Some dinosaur bones are huge. When they first discovered these fossilized bones, scientists imagined a terrifying prehistoric world full of house-size iguanas and crocodiles as big as elephants. These animals were so frightful they were given the Greek name "dinosaur," which means "fearfully great lizard."

Dinosaurs are indeed similar to iguanas and crocodiles, because, like living reptiles, they had scaly skin and laid eggs. Yet they are different from living reptiles in important ways.

First of all, many dinosaurs were *big*. Some of them were the largest animals ever to walk the Earth.

Second, dinosaurs are known for living in a period of time called the Mesozoic era. They appeared in the first part of the Mesozoic—called the Triassic period—about 230 million years ago. They dominated the earth through the Jurassic period and the last part of the Mesozoic—the Cretaceous period. A major extinction event at the end of the Cretaceous period 65 million years ago had a great impact on many forms of life, including dinosaurs.

Most important, dinosaurs were built differently from living reptiles. This caused them to move differently, too. Have you ever seen how living reptiles, such as lizards or turtles, walk with their bellies close to the ground and their limbs spread out to the sides of their bodies? Well, unlike all other reptiles, dinosaurs kept their legs tucked underneath their bodies, not out to the side, and their feet close together. The earliest-known dinosaurs moved almost entirely on their hind limbs. Their bone structure and muscles were designed exclusively for two-legged locomotion—like ours. This is called being bipedal.

Because they walked on their hind limbs, bipedal dinosaurs were free to do other things with their forelimbs. They used their free hands for grasping and grabbing. Some even had a dinosaur "thumb." Unique features like these caused the British naturalist Sir Richard Owen to set the "fearfully great lizards" in a group of their own called Dinosauria.

From these early bipedal dinosaurs emerged the hundreds of different species of dinosaurs that are known today. Many of the larger dinosaurs became

Many dinosaurs, like this tyrannosaur on display in a museum, were very big reptiles.

plant-eaters and began walking on four legs. Some groups grew very long necks and tails. Others grew horns or plates of bony armor. But some dinosaurs, including the meat-eaters, remained bipedal throughout the Mesozoic era.

Most scientists in the 1800s saw birds as completely different from—not closely related to—reptiles. They kept them in a category all their own called Aves. They pointed to "avian"—or birdlike—features such as their toothless beaks, arms used as wings for flying, and their small size to justify placing birds in their own animal group. Their strongest argument for this, however, was that birds possessed something that no other creature in the animal kingdom had—feathers.

In 1860, a German scientist announced the discovery of a fossil feather in a slab of 145-million-year-old limestone. He named the animal the feather had come from *Archaeopteryx*, which means "ancient feather" or "ancient wing." A nearly complete skeleton with the impressions of many feathers was found soon after.

Archaeopteryx was obviously a clue

Dinosaurs may have shared more than skeletal features with birds. New evidence suggests many of them shared feather-like structures, perhaps like those imagined for this hatchling Tyrannosaurus rex.

11

to the mystery of bird origins, but scientists could not agree on what the clue meant. If *Archaeopteryx* had been found without its feathers preserved, it might have been classified as a small dinosaur. In fact, one specimen of *Archaeopteryx* found in 1950 was misidentified as the dinosaur *Compsognathus*, because no feathers were preserved. The presence of feathers on the original fossil, however, led Sir Richard Owen, the scientist who came up with the group name Dinosauria, to reject its connection to reptiles. He placed it firmly in the group Aves as the most primitive bird known to science.

Feathers on the fossil of Archaeopteryx *(opposite) were the main reason for classifying it as a bird and not as a reptile like the pterosaur shown with* Archaeopteryx *above.*

In the many years since the discovery of this oldest-known bird, scientists have come to agree that all birds did, in fact, descend from reptiles. Among the features in today's birds that remind us of their reptilian ancestry are their scaly legs and the fact that they laid eggs. Before the 1970s, a few scientists argued that birds evolved from dinosaurs, but most thought they came from a different branch of the evolutionary tree.

But then things changed. In 1973, John Ostrom, a paleontologist at Yale University in Connecticut, was comparing the bones of *Deinonychus*, a small meat-eating dinosaur, with the skeleton of *Archaeopteryx*. He thought that the skeleton of *Deinonychus*, even though it was as big as that of an adult human, looked amazingly like a bird's. This led him to suggest that small carnivorous dinosaurs might be the ancestors of birds.

Dinosaur Babies and Birds

Imagine a field of eggs a football field long. The eggs are so densely packed on the ground that everywhere you stepped you would crunch eggshells. That's exactly what scientists are finding in places as far apart as Montana, Argentina, and France. But these eggs aren't alive. These eggs are millions of years old! They are the fossil remains of the giant nesting grounds of dinosaurs. From discoveries like these, scientists are learning that some dinosaurs behaved a lot like birds.

How can you study the behavior of animals that are extinct? It's not easy, but with good detective work in fossil sites such as the egg fields, scientists can figure out how dinosaurs behaved.

For example, big dinosaur nesting sites suggest that some dinosaurs lived in large groups—at least part of the time. In that way, they were like some birds, such as penguins, that nest together by the hundreds. Dinosaur tracks show us that groups of dinosaurs traveled together. At the Davenport Ranch site in Texas, parallel

Dinosaur parents such as these duck-billed dinosaurs may have nested together in large numbers and cared for their young much the way birds do.

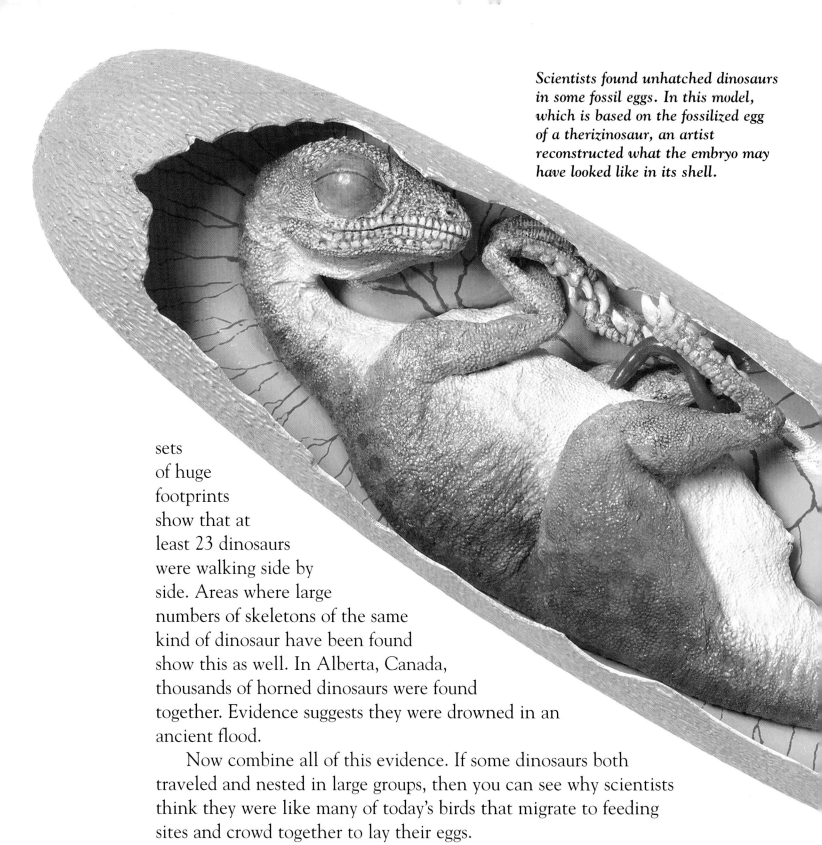

Scientists found unhatched dinosaurs in some fossil eggs. In this model, which is based on the fossilized egg of a therizinosaur, an artist reconstructed what the embryo may have looked like in its shell.

sets of huge footprints show that at least 23 dinosaurs were walking side by side. Areas where large numbers of skeletons of the same kind of dinosaur have been found show this as well. In Alberta, Canada, thousands of horned dinosaurs were found together. Evidence suggests they were drowned in an ancient flood.

Now combine all of this evidence. If some dinosaurs both traveled and nested in large groups, then you can see why scientists think they were like many of today's birds that migrate to feeding sites and crowd together to lay their eggs.

Paleontologists have found individual fossil nests containing groups—or clutches—of eggs at some of these dinosaur nesting grounds. From them scientists can draw conclusions about how

Fossil dinosaur eggs have been discovered in clutches, like the one from Argentina (above, left). These are similar to the nests of some living birds, such as the ostrich nest shown above, right.

dinosaurs behaved as parents and what baby dinosaurs were like. And it turns out that some were very much like birds.

In the 1920s, the skeleton of a dinosaur was found lying on top of a clutch of fossil eggs in Mongolia. Scientists thought the dinosaur was stealing the eggs of another dinosaur and named it *Oviraptor philoceratops*—"predator that loves to eat the eggs of horned dinosaurs." In the 1990s, expeditions led by the American Museum of Natural History discovered more specimens like this. Among the many fossil eggs discovered, paleontologists found some with well-preserved fossilized embryos—unhatched dinosaurs—inside. To their surprise, the embryos were of *Oviraptor*, not horned dinosaurs! Clearly the adult *Oviraptor* had died while incubating or protecting its own eggs the way bird parents do today. These and other fossil dinosaur embryos, along with bones of newly

Were dinosaurs born helpless like this newly hatched condor (near right)? Or were they able to get up and go like baby alligators (far right) and other living reptiles? Scientists are learning that some baby dinosaurs behaved like alligators, but others, like the duck-billed dinosaur shown in the model below, stayed in their nests and were cared for by their parents until they were strong enough to fend for themselves.

hatched dinosaurs, tell us something about the lives of baby dinosaurs.

Living reptiles such as turtles and alligators lay their eggs in a clutch and usually leave them alone to hatch. As soon as the young are born, they look much like miniature adults and can take care of themselves. In contrast, most baby birds require parental care for safety, food, and warmth. Some, like the songbirds, are born quite helpless. They have no feathers and are blind, and their bones are not strong enough for them to stand.

Paleontologist Jack Horner and his colleagues, working at a site

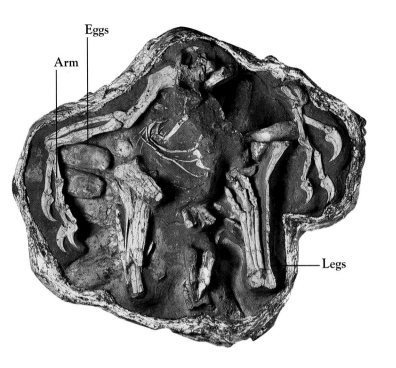

Eggs

Arm

Legs

A fossil discovered in Mongolia (near left) shows an adult Oviraptor on top of its nest. Perhaps it was protecting its young like the ostrich shown above. Scraps of food found in other nests suggest that parents fed their young in the nest, as shown in the art at far left.

called Egg Mountain in Montana, took what they knew about living animals and compared it with the fossil bones of dinosaur embryos and hatchlings. They found that some baby dinosaurs, including troodontids, were probably ready to leave the nest when they hatched, just like living reptiles and large birds such as ostriches. Other babies, including those of duck-billed dinosaurs, were born with poorly developed leg joints. It would have been hard for them to walk when they were first born, just as it is for some nestling birds.

Horner also found that baby duck-billed dinosaurs grew extremely fast—as baby birds do. The young dinosaurs went from sixteen inches long to nine feet long in one year! This is similar to the growth rate of ostriches and some other big birds. In contrast, an alligator only grows from one foot to three feet in its first year.

So it appears that dinosaurs had a variety of approaches to raising their young, some of which are shared only with living birds. Not all dinosaurs that show evidence of birdlike behavior and growth patterns were closely related to birds. But studying the behavior of *all* dinosaurs helps us understand where birds might have obtained some of their features in the first place.

Like a Bird from Head to Tail

So we know that some dinosaurs may have acted like birds, but we will never be completely sure about their behavior. Let's look at something we can be sure of—their bones.

Did you know that ostriches, parrots, and pelicans have given their names to dinosaurs? The bones of *Struthiomimus*, the ostrich mimic; *Psittacosaurus*, the parrot lizard; and *Pelicanimimus*, the pelican mimic, are just a few of the dinosaur fossils that reminded scientists so much of birds that they gave them avian names.

When studying dinosaur skeletons, scientists have found that although some groups of dinosaurs are only somewhat similar to birds, others share more than 100 specific skeletal features. One group of dinosaurs that has a lot in common with birds is the theropods. These are fast-running animals that include *Allosaurus*, *Tyrannosaurus*, *Deinonychus*, and all other meat-eating dinosaurs.

At first glance, today's cassowary (right) looks similar to an Oviraptor (above). Scientists dig deeper than surface appearances, however, to study the true links between dinosaurs and birds.

In the shadow of their preys' huge bodies, a pair of allosaurs stalk a herd of huge brachiosaurs. Theropods such as allosaurs share their three-toed feet with birds. Their tracks look a lot like bird footprints. The tracks above were found near Cameron, Arizona.

The name theropod—"beast foot"— comes from the big, nasty claws on their toes. All theropods walked on three large toes and had a small inner toe, called a hallux. Among dinosaurs, only theropod and ornithopod—"bird foot"—dinosaurs share this feature. Bird feet have the same unique structure, but in most birds the hallux is opposite the front three toes and used for grasping branches.

Although other groups of dinosaurs, such as the long-legged sauropods and

the horned dinosaurs, shifted to walking on all fours, theropods remained bipedal. They had long, powerful legs; slender arms; and a body balanced at the hip by a long tail.

Within the theropod group there are some dinosaurs that are the most birdlike of all: the maniraptors. Maniraptors include dromaeosaurs and troodontids. In a classification system accepted by most paleontologists, birds are maniraptors as well.

Dromaeosaurs and troodontids are fast predators best known for the sickle-shaped killing claw on their second toe. Dromaeosaurs and troodontids come in a wide range of sizes. Some are the size of hawks, but others are 25 feet long! *Velociraptor* and *Deinonychus*—both medium-size animals—are perhaps the best known of the dromaeosaurs. The best-known troodontid is *Troodon*, which gave the group its name.

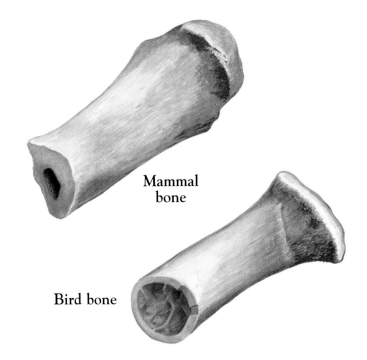

Mammal bone

Bird bone

Imagine the Wright brothers, inventors of the airplane, trying to take off with a plane loaded with rocks. The bones of dinosaurs and birds are thin-walled and remarkably light when compared with those of other animals. A light skeleton allowed big dinosaurs such as Tyrannosaurus rex (left) to run fast, and eventually made it possible for birds to launch into the air.

Both birds and other maniraptors have long arms. Without long arms—or wings—birds could not fly. The bones in these arms, as well as other bones of maniraptors, are lightweight. The wall of bone that surrounds the marrow is very thin.

The skulls of dromaeosaurs and troodontids are built with very little bone as well. They look like networks of holes held together by bony bridges. Some of the skull bones have balloon-like air sacs in them. Bird skulls have the same airy construction. These light bones reduced weight, perhaps allowing maniraptors to be quick. Eventually these lightweight bones made it easier for birds to fly.

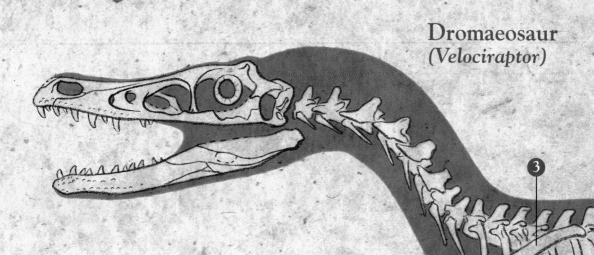

Dromaeosaur
(Velociraptor)

Under the skin of dinosaurs and birds

When scientists say birds are descended from dinosaurs they are talking about how birds are more similar to dinosaurs than to any other creatures, living or dead. They base this claim on similarities in the skeletons of dinosaurs and living birds. Studies show that birds and some groups of dinosaurs share more than 100 features. New features are frequently added to the list, as wishbones were when this V-shaped Velociraptor wishbone (below) was discovered in Mongolia in 1991.

COMPARING DINOSAURS AND BIRDS

1 Wishbone and 2 breastbone. Many theropods are now known to have wishbones as well as breastbones—both seen in birds living today.

3 Shoulder blade. Birds and theropods have long, thin shoulder blades.

4 Swiveling wrists. Unique bones allow the hands to fold against the lower arm and body.

5 Hand design. Both birds and maniraptors have lost two of their five fingers. There is some dispute about whether birds and

Crow

theropods lost the *same* two fingers. Of the three that remain, the middle is longest in both birds and maniraptors.

6 **Bone mass.** Birds and theropods have hollow, thin-walled bones.

7 **Pubis.** The pubic bone of the pelvis extends forward in most dinosaurs, and backward in birds and some theropods.

8 **Legs.** Birds and theropods are bipedal.

9 **Feet.** Birds and theropods have three forward-pointing toes and a hallux.

Hallux

Hallux

29

An inside look at wings

Just like your own arm, a bird's wing is made up of an upper arm, a forearm, and a hand. The same is true of bats and flying reptiles like extinct pterosaurs. Bat and pterosaur fingers became extremely long and—like kites—supported sheets of skin. The fingers of birds are reduced in number and modified. And they do not use skin to stay aloft, but instead use long, stiff feathers that extend from their arms and hands.

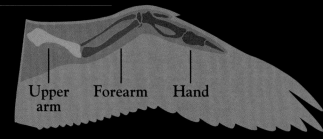

Upper arm   Forearm   Hand

Bird wing

Pterosaur wing

Bat wing

Scientists have found even more similarities in the skeletons of birds and other maniraptors. All land vertebrates have a set of bones called the "shoulder girdle" that attaches the arms to various muscles and the rib cage. Birds and other maniraptors share a shoulder girdle that allows great flexibility in the arms. Only dromaeosaurs, however, could raise their arms out to their sides like birds. Some could even move them down and forward in a flapping motion.

The shoulder blade—or scapula—is a part of the shoulder girdle. In humans the scapula is triangular. You can feel it if you reach behind your shoulders. But in birds and other theropods the scapula is shaped like a long, thin blade. In birds, this shape provides a large area for the attachment of muscles important for flight. The coracoid, a bone that attaches to the scapula, forms the shoulder joint with it. In some maniraptors, the coracoid connects to the breastbone and braces the shoulder as it moves, just as it does in a bird.

The wishbone—or furcula—and the breastbone—or sternum—are two other parts connected to the shoulder girdle that have unique shapes in birds. Until recently these bones were thought to belong only to birds. But now similar wishbones and breastbones

have been found on many theropods. Like the scapula, the furcula and sternum provide important areas for muscle attachment and structural support for the flight stroke of birds.

A maniraptor's wrist is perhaps its most birdlike feature. Birds and other maniraptors have a unique half-moon-shaped wrist bone that allows them to swivel their hands to the side and fold their arms and hands against their bodies. Birds use this motion in flight to move themselves forward.

But dromaeosaurs and troodontids did not fly. Why would they have such a specialized bunch of bones? This arm motion could have been used to give them a sudden burst of speed while running. Other evidence suggests that these animals used their strong, flexible arms and wrists to hunt. They could extend their arms and whip out their hands quickly to snatch prey, sort of like a gunslinger drawing a gun. Some scientists studying the origins of flight in birds suggest that the flight stroke of a bird began in the flexible arm motions of earlier maniraptors.

All of these similar features lead most paleontologists to conclude that birds are closely related to dromaeosaurs and troodontids. They think these quick, bipedal dinosaurs with their lightweight bones and long, flexible arms set the stage for flight.

Increasing evidence shows that the prey-grabbing motion of a dinosaur's arms is like the flight stroke of a bird. Early feathers may have been useful for extra balance or to boost jumping. Eventually dinosaurs became airborne as they leaped for prey.

Birdlike dinosaurs also may have climbed trees and become flyers as they jumped or glided down. We'll probably never know whether flight evolved from the ground or in trees. The important thing is how the flight stroke evolved.

The New Dinosaurs

If birds evolved from dinosaurs, then at some stage dinosaurs had to start growing feathers. But how and when did that happen? Feathers are so rarely preserved as fossils that for a long time no one expected to find a sure answer to this question. Then the unexpected happened.

In 1996 and 1997, some amazing discoveries were made at a fossil quarry in China's Liaoning Province. A large lake system covered this area about 124 million years ago. Every so often volcanoes erupted and buried creatures under layers of fine mud and ash. Over time, these layers of sediment turned to stone and preserved the buried animals as fossils. Now the ancient lake bed lies under green fields and can be reached by a little digging—something the farmers do frequently. Along with fish, turtles, mammals,

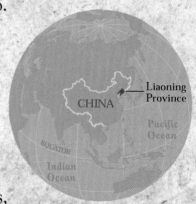

Fossils from Liaoning Province in China are sometimes so well preserved that details—such as the feather-like structures along the head, neck, and back of this fossil of Sinosauropteryx—are clearly visible.

and bugs, farmers found the skeletons of three theropods. Their bones were perfectly preserved on slabs of fine stone. And, to everyone's surprise, so were the remains of feather-like structures and true feathers!

This was the first time in history that feathers had been found on any animal—living or extinct—except a bird. The discovery rocked the scientific world. Scientists had already convincingly argued that birds and theropods were closely related. Now they knew theropods had feathers, too. The conclusion was obvious: Theropods must be the ancestors of birds, and birds—

A feathery family

Feathers and other skin coverings seem to be widespread in the group of dinosaurs called theropods. Shown here are some theropods that may have had feathers, as well as other well-known ones. They are arranged from left to right in order of their closeness to birds. They are not arranged according to when they lived.

If theropods like Sinosauropteryx *had feather-like structures or some other skin covering, then it is possible that related theropods, including* Tyrannosaurus rex *and* Velociraptor, *had feathers or similar structures at some stage in their lives, too. In the same way that parents pass on features to offspring, feathers could have been passed on to descendants of the first feathered creature.*

Tyrannosaurus rex
Probably more advanced than *Sinosauropteryx*. Did *T. rex* young have feather-like structures?

THEROPODS FARTHER FROM BIRDS

Sinosauropteryx
Feather-like structures

Unnamed oviraptor
Pygostyle suggests feathered tail

36

even cardinals, blue jays, and sparrows—must be flying theropods.

Within the last few years, even more theropods with feather-like structures have been found in China. *Sinosauropteryx*, *Protarchaeopteryx*, and *Caudipteryx*, the first of these new dinosaurs to be discovered, reached the size of turkeys. But others, like *Beipiaosaurus*, were as big as a ostriches. The coverings of these dinosaurs ranged from a short hairlike coat to long feathers similar to those you might see on a living bird's tail.

What surprises many scientists is that these feathery creatures

Sinornithosaurus
Feather-like structures

Velociraptor
Very close to birds.
Did it have feathers, too?

THEROPODS CLOSER TO BIRDS | BIRDS

Caudipteryx
Feathers and feather-like structures, but flightless

Beipiaosaurus
Feather-like structures

Protarchaeopteryx
Feathers and feather-like structures, but flightless

Archaeopteryx
Flight feathers

are spread throughout the theropod group. They include dromaeosaurs, therizinosaurs, oviraptorids, and others. This suggests that feathers may have been a common feature among theropods.

This is a startling idea. Because they're all closely related, it's possible that well-known dinosaurs like *Tyrannosaurus*, *Deinonychus*, *Oviraptor*, and *Velociraptor* all had feathers or feather-like structures, at least at some stage of their lives.

Several fossils of Sinosauropteryx (above, left) have been found since the first was discovered in 1996. Each fossil has areas covered with what appear to be downlike feathers, such as those shown magnified at bottom left. Although some scientists search for other explanations, most agree that this material is most likely the remains of a feathery coat.

So, from this one area in China, the world has not just one answer to the question of which dinosaur started to grow feathers, but many! Let's see what these newly discovered feathered dinosaurs looked like.

If you could travel back in time 124 million years to the ancient lake in what is now China's Liaoning Province, you might catch a glimpse of chicken-size *Sinosauropteryx* hunting along the water's edge. You might even be lucky enough to see it pounce on a lizard or gobble up a small mammal that came for a drink. We know it ate these things, because some specimens of this animal are so well preserved that we can see their last meals in their stomachs.

Sinosauropteryx—which means "Chinese lizard feather"— created a worldwide sensation when Chinese scientists attending a conference showed some photographs of what appeared to be the remains of a dense coat of hairlike fibers.

Sinosauropteryx is also the most primitive of the dinosaurs recently discovered at Liaoning. Unlike

Sinosauropteryx prima
"ancient Chinese dragon feather"

Caudipteryx zhoui
"feathered tail of Zhou"

A close-up inspection of the fossil of Caudipteryx reveals the distinct impression of true feathers.

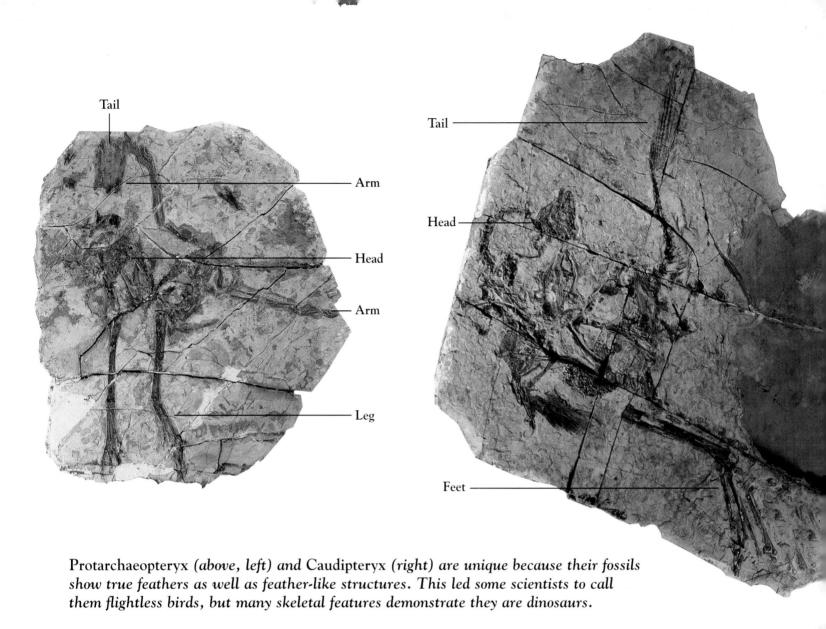

Tail

Arm

Head

Arm

Leg

Tail

Head

Feet

Protarchaeopteryx *(above, left) and* **Caudipteryx** *(right) are unique because their fossils show true feathers as well as feather-like structures. This led some scientists to call them flightless birds, but many skeletal features demonstrate they are dinosaurs.*

more advanced theropods such as dromaeosaurs, it had very short arms and a long tail. Its primitive shoulder girdle would not allow it to flap its arms. The presence of a downy covering on a primitive theropod like *Sinosauropteryx* suggests that a covering of this type appeared early in the evolution of theropods, perhaps as a way to keep warm, or for camouflage.

Soon after the discovery of *Sinosauropteryx*, two other feathered but flightless dinosaurs were found. They both had the feather-like covering seen on *Sinosauropteryx*, but they also had longer feathers similar to those we see on birds today. One was named *Caudipteryx* and the other *Protarchaeopteryx*. *Caudipteryx* had a beak like

41

Oviraptor but had a few tiny teeth at the end of its beak. Unfortunately the head of *Protarchaeopteryx* was poorly preserved.

Both animals had feathers on their hands and a fan of plumage on their tails as well. Though their feathers probably made them look like birds, the skeletons of *Caudipteryx* and *Protarchaeopteryx* make it clear that they were nonflying dinosaurs. Scientists are still studying which other theropods these two dinosaurs are most closely related to.

Even though they look quite a bit like the feathers of flying birds today, the long symmetrical feathers on these dinosaurs are not suitable for flight. So they must have served some other purpose. Perhaps these dinosaurs used their feathery tails as a display to attract mates or to warn enemies.

Sinornithosaurus is a close relative of *Velociraptor* and the first dromaeosaur found with feather-like structures. In some ways *Sinornithosaurus* is the most birdlike feathered dinosaur yet found, because it could flap its arms! Its shoulders were angled so that they could lift the arms well above the head. Its shoulder girdle is so similar to that

Sinornithosaurus milenii
"Chinese bird reptile of the millennium"

42

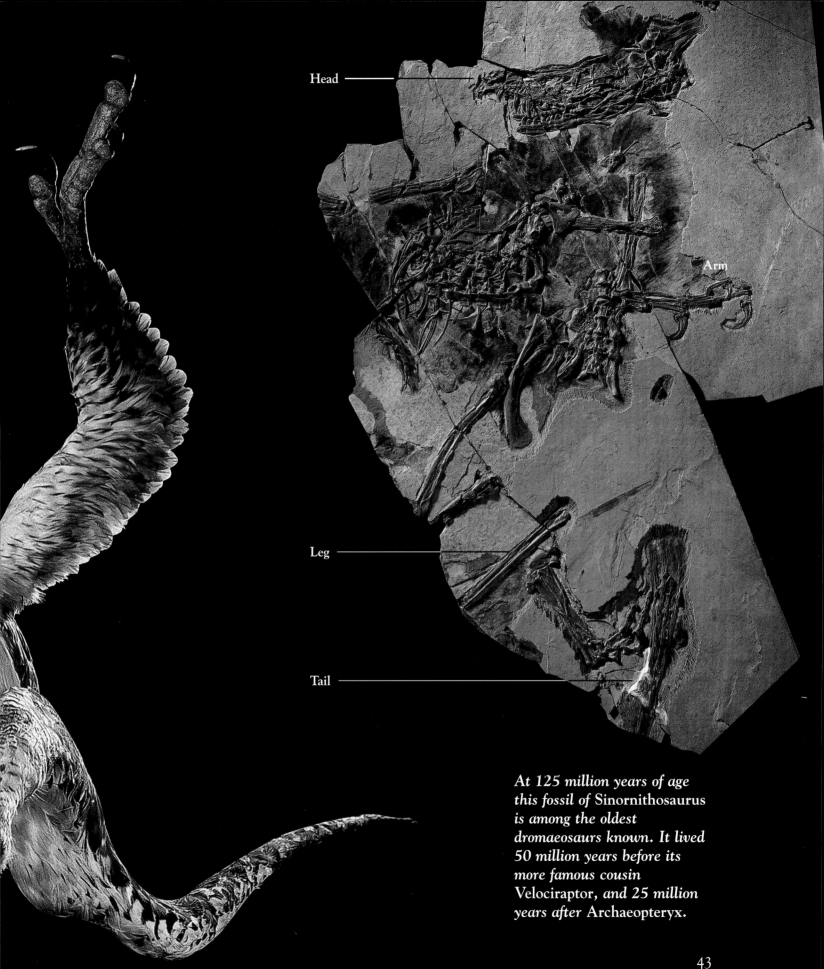

Head

Arm

Leg

Tail

At 125 million years of age this fossil of Sinornithosaurus is among the oldest dromaeosaurs known. It lived 50 million years before its more famous cousin Velociraptor, and 25 million years after Archaeopteryx.

43

Chinese scientist Xu Xing carefully prepares the fossil skeleton of Beipiaosaurus *(left). The long strands of hairlike material on the fossil, shown near life size at right, may be the remains of feathers.*

of *Archaeopteryx* that it would be easy to confuse the two. *Sinornithosaurus* also had long birdlike arms that were almost as long as its legs. But the big jaws of *Sinornithosaurus* show that it had a mouth filled with dagger-like teeth. There's no mistaking them for the tiny teeth of a toothed bird.

A halo of inch-long hairlike structures surrounds the fossil skeleton of *Sinornithosaurus*, suggesting that in life it was completely covered with them. Some scientists think if it had had true feathers like those of *Archaeopteryx*, it could have flown.

Beipiaosaurus is the biggest of the newly discovered dinosaurs. It is a seven-foot-long creature belonging to a group of dinosaurs called therizinosaurs. Therizinosaurs are known for their long necks, tiny teeth, and long claws on their hands. Their small teeth suggest they ate fish, insects, or even plants. Perhaps they used their long claws to catch fish, tear down foliage, or dig into anthills.

One thing the discovery of *Beipiaosaurus* helped to confirm was that therizinosaurs are theropods. *Beipiaosaurus* had the same birdlike skeleton as other theropods. It also had long, skinny fibers that formed a three-inch fringe along its arms. And so far, theropods are the only group of dinosaurs found with these feather-like structures!

Crow

Beipiaosaurus

The First Feathers

In 1860, a month or two before the discovery of the first skeleton of *Archaeopteryx*, the impression of a lone fossil feather was found in a slab of limestone in Bavaria, Germany. Scientists were stunned by the fossil because it was the same shape as a living bird's feather, yet they knew it must be very old. This meant that flying birds existed millions of years before previously thought.

The fossil feather of *Archaeopteryx* is remarkable because it is asymmetrical—it is not even on both sides of the shaft. This gives a feather

The shape of the Archaeopteryx *feather (left) shows that the earliest-known bird could fly. But feathers may have evolved for a variety of purposes besides flight, such as keeping warm or attracting mates. Attracting a mate is the only purpose of a fancy peacock feather (right).*

46

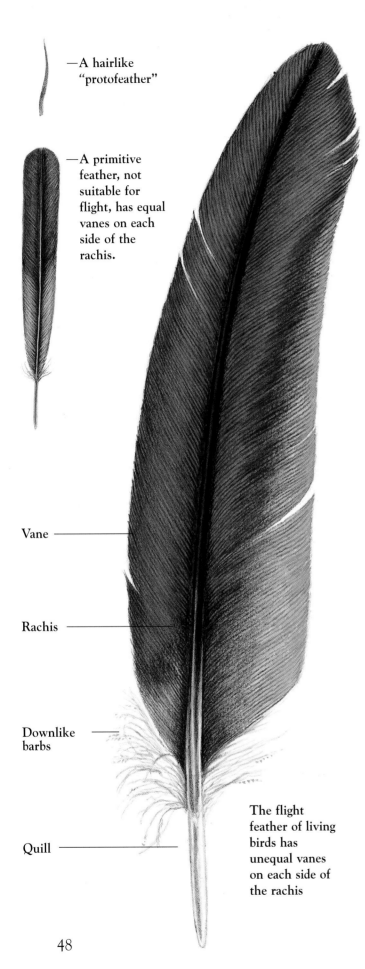

—A hairlike "protofeather"

—A primitive feather, not suitable for flight, has equal vanes on each side of the rachis.

Vane

Rachis

Downlike barbs

Quill

The flight feather of living birds has unequal vanes on each side of the rachis

Feather expert Dr. Alan Brush (right) suggests that feathers may have passed through several evolutionary stages before gaining their modern appearance. The earliest feathers—or protofeathers—may have been hairlike, creating an appearance much like that of today's kiwi (above).

an "air foil" shape in cross-section—the same shape that engineers give to an airplane wing to create lift. Though most scientists look at *Archaeopteryx*'s skeleton and think it wasn't much of a flier compared with birds today, they agree that its wings and asymmetrical feathers were likely used for flight.

Today's birds display a multitude of feather colors and types. Some are used for flight, of course, but others are used to help birds communicate and recognize one another. Feathers of dull color are useful as camouflage for hiding. Brightly colored feathers are used to attract mates. Some birds, such

as turkeys and peacocks, use a fan of long tail feathers to impress the opposite sex. Feathers protect a bird's skin from scratches and even repel water.

Until the discovery of the feathered dinosaurs, there was no fossil evidence of what early feathers looked like. Scientists who study feathers had proposed that there were "protofeathers"—first feathers—before modern feathers evolved. They thought protofeathers were hairlike or simple branching feathers similar in appearance to the feathers that can be found on many living birds. Turkey vultures, for example, have short, thin feathers on their heads, and the feathers of kiwis are very hairlike as well. It is also common for birds to have hairlike feather "eyelashes" near their eyes.

The structures on *Sinosauropteryx* have also been compared to a soft, fluffy type of feather called down on chicks and adult birds. Many scientists agree that, because of their hairlike or

49

downlike appearance and their position on the fossils, the structures seen on *Sinosauropteryx* and other feathered dinosaurs might be protofeathers that later evolved into true feathers.

These skin coverings probably protected the dinosaurs from extremes of heat and cold. Feathers and fur, in fact, are two of the best insulators known. Insulators, like the insulation in the walls of your home, prevent rapid heat gain or loss. Down is an especially good insulator. It can trap a layer of air near the body and keep the skin from direct contact with the cold.

There is good reason to think that ground-dwelling dinosaurs, like living birds, used feathers for many purposes. The feathers on *Caudipteryx* and *Protarchaeopteryx*, for example, had gone beyond being simple and hairlike. They had a shaft and vanes, like many feathers today, but were symmetrical. Perhaps they were used for display or to cover eggs while the dinosaur was sitting on a nest.

Tern nestlings (above, left) use their down for warmth and camouflage. A heron (above) has long feathers on its wings that help make it a strong flier. The fringe of feathers on the head of a monkey-eating eagle (right) or in the fan of a roadrunner's tail (below) is effective in making these birds look fierce—or attractive.

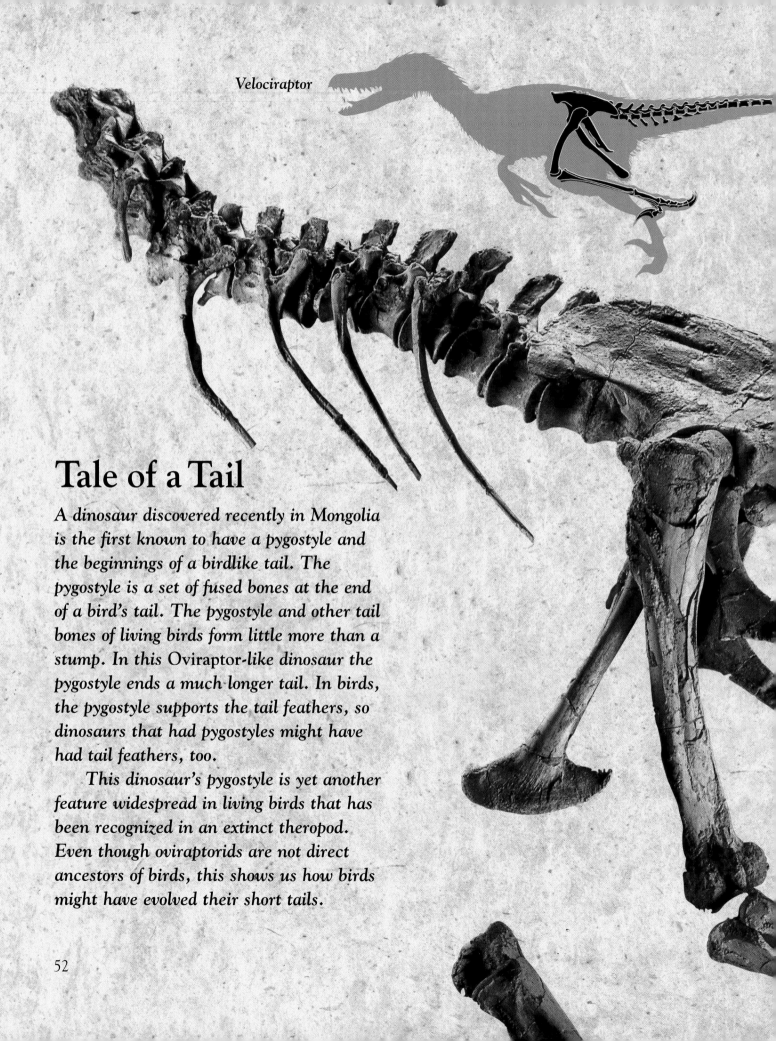

Tale of a Tail

A dinosaur discovered recently in Mongolia is the first known to have a pygostyle and the beginnings of a birdlike tail. The pygostyle is a set of fused bones at the end of a bird's tail. The pygostyle and other tail bones of living birds form little more than a stump. In this Oviraptor-like dinosaur the pygostyle ends a much longer tail. In birds, the pygostyle supports the tail feathers, so dinosaurs that had pygostyles might have had tail feathers, too.

This dinosaur's pygostyle is yet another feature widespread in living birds that has been recognized in an extinct theropod. Even though oviraptorids are not direct ancestors of birds, this shows us how birds might have evolved their short tails.

Eagle

Pygostyle

Pygostyle

Most long-tailed theropods, such as Velociraptor (above, left), had 30 to 40 bones—or vertebrae—in their tails. The unnamed Oviraptor-like dinosaur (left and below) shows signs of a shortening of the tail to 19 movable vertebrae plus a pygostyle. In comparison, an eagle's tail has six vertebrae and a pygostyle.

Unnamed Oviraptor-like dinosaur

Pygostyle

The Early Birds

For 100 years after the discovery of *Archaeopteryx*, not much was known of birds that lived in the era of dinosaurs. But in the last 20 years, paleontologists have discovered many early birds that shed light on where today's birds came from.

What they learned is that birds that came after *Archaeopteryx* made a slow transformation into their living forms. Over millions of years, sharp teeth were lost and replaced by horny beaks. Long, bony, dinosaurian tails shortened until not much more than the pygostyle was left. The breastbone, small in *Archaeopteryx*, increased in size to become one of the largest bones in a bird's body. And their brains got bigger, partly to help them with the complexities of air travel.

If you went back in time to the ancient lake in Liaoning, you would see lots of *Confuciusornis* birds flying from tree to tree. They were more similar to today's birds than *Archaeopteryx* was. Like *Archaeopteryx*, *Confuciusornis* had claws on its wings, but it did not have a long reptilian tail. Instead of teeth, it had a horny sheath we call a beak. It is the earliest beaked bird known.

Early birds' clawed fingers eventually gave way to finger bones

Scientists are not sure how well the earliest bird known, Archaeopteryx, *flew. As birds became better flyers, they lost their hand claws, long reptilian tails, and even their teeth.*

that first became smaller and then changed shape to reduce the need for large muscles to hold the fingers together during flight.

Although other fingers changed, the thumb stayed separate and supported a small feathered "thumb wing" called the alula. Birds use their alula to control the amount of air passing over their wings. This helps them avoid stalling in midair when they need to slow down.

All of these changes in birds occurred during the time of the dinosaurs. There is now quite a bit of evidence that primitive forms of many birds, such as shorebirds, ducks, loons, and albatross relatives, originated before the great extinction of the nonflying dinosaurs about 65 million years ago. Some bird groups—including all of the toothed birds—died out along with the nonflying dinosaurs.

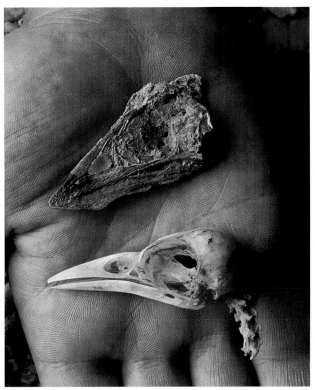

The beaked fossil skull of Confuciusornis, *above, is compared with an oriole skull. Although this primitive bird is best known for its beak, it also had a dramatic display of long tail feathers (left).*

Scientists are still studying the reasons for the great extinction at the end of the Cretaceous period 65 million years ago. An asteroid impact is a strong possibility, but without a firm idea of the cause, it's impossible to say why some bird groups flew into modern times and others did not.

Some scientists argue that birds didn't descend from dinosaurs. One of their main objections is that if feathered dinosaurs were the ancestors of birds, how could the bird *Archaeopteryx* have been flying around 25 million years before these other feathered dinosaurs lived? At first glance, this does seem backward.

From arms to wings

A bird's wing is a very complicated structure. Evidence shows that the features of a bird's wing that are related to flight evolved piece by piece, not all at once. Several of the important features evolved in nonflying animals.

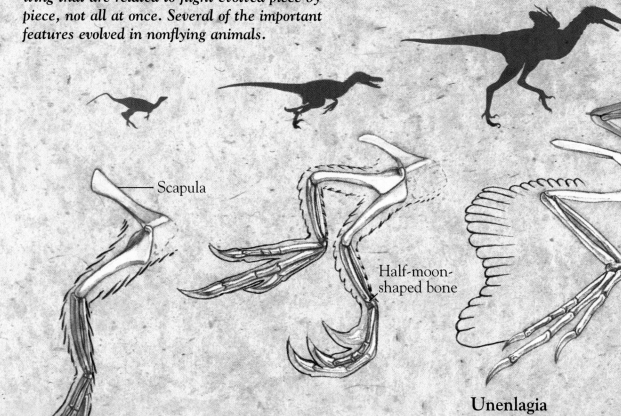

Scapula

Half-moon-shaped bone

Sinosauropteryx

A ground-dwelling dinosaur with short arms and three-fingered hands, Sinosauropteryx had typical theropod arms. "What appear to be downlike feathers covered its body. Its long scapula is similar to the bladelike scapula of birds.

Velociraptor

A half-moon-shaped bone in the wrist of dromaeosaurs such as Velociraptor made it possible for them to swivel their wrists to the side. This flexibility also allowed them to fold their arms against their bodies like a bird. These motions, which may have been useful for catching prey, were later incorporated into a bird's flight stroke. No fossil evidence of feathers exists for Velociraptor, but Sinornithosaurus—a close relative—is covered in downlike material.

Unenlagia

Specially shaped shoulder bones allowed Unenlagia, an ostrich-size creature found Argentina, to raise its arms above its head. Dr. Fernando Novas, a scientist who studied Unenlagia, suggests that it may have raised its arms for balance as it ran, somewhat like a surfer balancing on a surfboard. Now new evidence suggests that other dromaeosaurs could also raise their arms as Unenlagia could. No fossil evidence of feathers exists for Unenlagia.

—Alula

Archaeopteryx

Archaeopteryx is the earliest-known flying bird. Its asymmetrical feathers are similar to those of today's flying birds. But its long arms still had claws, and other bones—including those of its small sternum and long tail—suggest that when it flew, it could not fly far.

Eoalulavis

An important step toward the wings of today's flying birds is present in Eoalulavis, a primitive bird discovered in Spain. Its thumb has developed into an important structure supporting the alula. The alula is a tuft of feathers attached to the thumb that living birds use to control the flow of air over the wing. This allows them to regulate flight at low speeds, such as during takeoffs and landings.

Crow

Flying birds of today, such as the crow, are excellent flying machines. Their huge wing surfaces, shortened tails, and large flight muscles attached to large sternums set them apart from their ancestors.

59

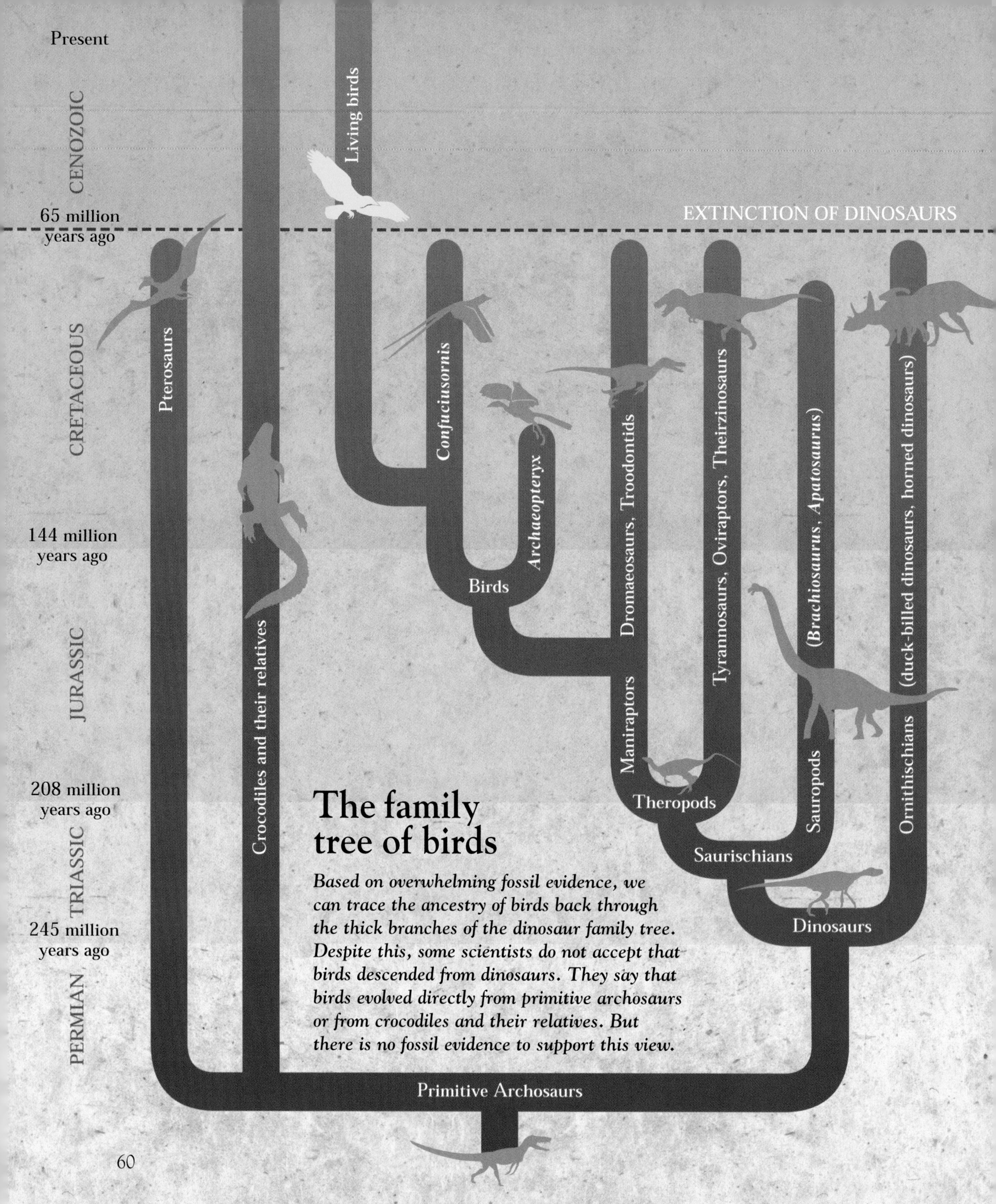

The family tree of birds

Based on overwhelming fossil evidence, we can trace the ancestry of birds back through the thick branches of the dinosaur family tree. Despite this, some scientists do not accept that birds descended from dinosaurs. They say that birds evolved directly from primitive archosaurs or from crocodiles and their relatives. But there is no fossil evidence to support this view.

Present

CENOZOIC

65 million years ago — EXTINCTION OF DINOSAURS

CRETACEOUS

144 million years ago

JURASSIC

208 million years ago

TRIASSIC

245 million years ago

PERMIAN

Living birds

Pterosaurs

Crocodiles and their relatives

Confuciusornis

Archaeopteryx

Birds

Maniraptors

Dromaeosaurs, Troodontids

Theropods

Tyrannosaurs, Oviraptors, Theirzinosaurs

Saurischians

Sauropods (Brachiosaurus, Apatosaurus)

Ornithischians (duck-billed dinosaurs, horned dinosaurs)

Dinosaurs

Primitive Archosaurs

When did living groups of birds originate? Dr. Luis Chiappe (above), who studies fossil birds, suggests that at least several of today's bird groups were living before the great dinosaur extinction.

The explanation supported by the most evidence is that the dinosaurs at Liaoning descended from an ancestor they shared with *Archaeopteryx*. This ancestor—probably a light-bodied, long-armed theropod that looked something like a small dromaeosaur—evolved feathers for reasons other than flight long before *Archaeopteryx* took to the air. This creature produced many feathery descendants. Some, such as *Archaeopteryx*, used their feathers to experiment with flight. Others, such as the dinosaurs at Liaoning, did not.

Now scientists are investigating new questions. If the dinosaur ancestors of birds were warm-blooded, how and when did the switch from cold-blooded to warm-blooded dinosaurs happen? When dinosaurs started to fly, did they take off by running on the ground or by jumping out of trees?

With mounting evidence that dinosaurs were the ancestors of birds, museum exhibits like this one in Utah are giving birdlike dinosaurs such as Deinonychus, *shown above, a feathery facelift.*

One of the biggest questions is: "What is a bird?" With so many features shared between dinosaurs and birds, the distinction between the two is blurry. Scientists are working hard to come up with a new definition of "bird" that everyone can agree on. One definition that seems to work is that a bird is *Archaeopteryx* and all the other animals closer to living birds. *Archaeopteryx* has been accepted as a true bird for 140 years, so this makes sense in many ways.

Birds are an important and beautiful part of our world. They have spread across the globe and diversified into more than 9,700 species. We enjoy them as bird-watchers, as friends, and even as Thanksgiving turkey-eaters! Perhaps they will seem even more important to you now that you know they're also dinosaurs!

Glossary

alula: A tuft of small feathers supported by the first digit, or thumb, of a bird's hand.

Aves: The group that contains all living and fossil birds, including *Archaeopteryx*.

avian: Relating to birds. The word comes from "Aves."

archosaur: A group of reptiles, including dinosaurs, pterosaurs, and crocodiles and their relatives. They first appeared at the end of the Permian period, about 245 million years ago.

bipedal: Walking or moving using only the back legs.

Cretaceous: The last period of the Mesozoic. It lasted from approximately 145 million years ago to 65 million years ago and ended with a great extinction.

coracoid: The bone of the shoulder girdle that connects to the scapula to form the shoulder joint. The coracoid sometimes connects with the sternum and furcula.

Dinosauria: The group that contains dinosaurs and their descendants. The word is Greek for "fearfully great lizards," but is more commonly translated as "terrible lizards."

dromaeosaur: A group of birdlike theropods that includes *Velociraptor* and *Deinonychus*. They are best known for having a large claw on their second toe and tails strengthened by rods.

furcula: The wishbone of a dinosaur or bird. It is formed by the fusion—or joining—of the two collar bones.

hallux: In birds and theropods the hallux is a reduced first toe. In most birds it is rotated and allows the foot to grasp a perch or prey.

Jurassic: The middle period of the Mesozoic that lasted from approximately 208 million years ago to 144 million years ago.

Mesozoic: The era best known as the age of dinosaurs. It has three periods; the Triassic, Jurassic, and Cretaceous. The Mesozoic lasted from 245 million years ago to 65 million years ago.

maniraptorans: A theropod group known for its long arms and unique wrist bone. The group includes dromaeosaurs, troodontids, and birds.

Ornithischia: One of two major divisions of dinosaurs, defined by their "birdlike" hips. Birds are *not* closely related to ornithischians, which include horned dinosaurs and duck-billed dinosaurs, among others.

oviraptorids: A group of theropods known for their beak-shaped toothless jaws.

paleontologist: A scientist who studies life of the past, using fossils and other evidence.

pterosaur: Extinct flying reptiles with skin that stretched between the body and long fourth finger.

pygostyle: A set of fused vertebrae that occur at the end of a bird's tail. The pygostyle supports tail feathers.

Saurischia: One of two major divisions of dinosaurs, defined by their traditional "lizard-like" hips. The group includes theropods and sauropods.

sauropod: A major group of four-legged, long-necked dinosaurs that includes the largest known land animals.

scapula: The shoulder blade.

shoulder girdle: A set of bones that includes the scapula, coracoid, and furcula. Together these bones form a structure critical for flight in birds.

sternum: A bone in the center of the chest that in birds has been enlarged to support strong muscles.

theropod: A large group of meat-eating dinosaurs that includes tyrannosaurids, oviraptorids, dromaeosaurs, troodontids, therizinosaurs, and birds, among others.

therizinosaurs: A group of long-necked theropods known for their long hand claws and small teeth.

Triassic: The first period of the Mesozoic, which lasted from approximately 245 million years ago to 208 million years ago.

troodontids: Small long-legged maniraptorans with large brains and retractable claws on their second toe.

vertebrae: Bones of the spine.

Index

Illustration credits

1: Photo by Farrell Grehan, art by Greg Paul. 2-3,4: Greg Paul. 5: Michael Skrepnick. 6: O. Louis Mazzatenta. 7: Greg Paul. 8: B. Anthony Stewart. 9: James L. Stanfield. 10-11: Michael Skrepnick. 12: Charles Knight. 13: O. Louis Mazzantenta. 14: John Gurche. 15: Greg Paul. 16-17: Model by Brian Cooley, photo by Mark Thiessen. 17: Left, Brooks Walker; right, Des and Jen Bartlett. 18: Top, Joel Sartore; bottom, model by Matt Smith, photo by Mark Thiessen. 19: Chris Johns. 20: John Sibbick. 21: Left, photo by D. Finnin, courtesy Department of Library Services, American Museum of Natural History; right, Des and Jen Bartlett. 22: Greg Paul. 23: Medford Taylor. 24-25: John Gurche. 25: George H. H. Huey. 26: Richard T. Nowitz. 27: Christopher Sloan. 28-29: Portia Sloan. 28: Bottom, photo by Mick Ellison, courtesy Department of Library Services, American Museum of Natural History. 30-31: Photo by O. Louis Mazzatenta, art by Christopher Sloan. 32-33: Mark Hallett. 34: O. Louis Mazzatenta. 35: Top, Greg Paul; bottom, Christopher Sloan. 36-37: Portia Sloan. 38-39: Model by Brian Cooley, photo by Mark Thiessen. 38: Top and bottom, O. Louis Mazzatenta. 40: Model by Brian Cooley, photos by O. Louis Mazzatenta. 41: O. Louis Mazzatenta. 42-45: Model by Brian Cooley, photos by O. Louis Mazzatenta, art by Christopher Sloan. 46: Top, Greg Paul; bottom, O. Louis Mazzatenta. 47: Todd Gipstein. 48: Art by Christopher Sloan, photo by Gregory Herbert. 49: O. Louis Mazzatenta. 50: Annie Griffiths Belt. 51: Top, Comstock; bottom left, Bruce Dale; bottom right, F.R.E.E., Ltd. 52-53: Photo by O. Louis Mazzatenta, art by Portia Sloan. 54: John Gurche. 55: Greg Paul. 56, 57: O. Louis Mazzatenta. 58-59: Portia Sloan. 60: Christopher Sloan. 61: O. Louis Mazzatenta. 62: O. Louis Mazzatenta. 63: Greg Paul

The world's largest nonprofit scientific and educational organization, the National Geographic Society was founded in 1888 "for the increase and diffusion of geographic knowledge." Fulfilling this mission, the Society educates and inspires millions everyday through magazines, books, television programs, videos, maps and atlases, research grants, the National Geographic Bee, teacher workshops, and innovative classroom materials.

Visit our website at www.nationalgeographic.com

The Society is supported through membership dues and income from the sale of its educational products. Call 1-800-NGS-LINE for more information.